Content

From the Editor

In this issue, we are proud to feature James Donaldson, NBA All-Star, successful entrepreneur, and community leader.

We also hear from personal branding expert, Phillip Lanos. Phillip is also the co-host of the wildly successful *War Room Moments* podcast series.

Melanie Kossan shares her experience in the CBD business and how she built a successful company in a heavily regulated industry.

Otis McGregor, retired US Army lieutenant colonel and elite Green Beret commander, shares incredible insight into tribe and purpose.

Julia Greenberg-Aguilar and Katerina Zuniga give us insight into the LLC, and Bob Bieneas helps us understand automated retailing.

Video and content expert, Kelli Maxwell, teaches content marketing, and Michael Sipe shares ten principles of servant leadership.

This issue is jam-packed with business goodness. I hope you enjoy reading it as much as I enjoyed putting it all together for you.

Chris O'Byrne
Editor-in-Chief

PIVOT Magazine

Founder and President
Jason Miller
jason@strategicadvisorboard.com

Editor-in-Chief
Chris O'Byrne
chris@jetlaunch.net

Design
JETLAUNCH.net

Advertising
Chris O'Byrne
chris@jetlaunch.net

Webmaster
Joel Phillips
joel@proshark.com

Editor
Laura West
laura@jetlaunch.net

James Donaldson
From NBA All-Star to Entrepreneur

James Donaldson played professional basketball in the NBA with the Seattle SuperSonics, San Diego/Los Angeles Clippers, Dallas Mavericks, New York Knicks, and Utah Jazz. He also played for several teams in the European Leagues in Spain, Italy, and Greece, and he toured with The Harlem Globetrotters to wrap up his career.

James was an NBA All-Star while playing center for the Dallas Mavericks. James was inducted into the PAC-10 Sports Hall of Fame and the Washington State University Athletic Hall of Fame. He was elected as a board member for the NBA Retired Players Association. He was also the recipient of the NBA Legends of Basketball ABC Award, awarded for outstanding contributions in Athletics–Business–Community.

Childhood

I grew up in south Sacramento in a diverse neighborhood. My father was in the military and then worked for the post office. My mother was a factory foreman. Nobody I knew was an entrepreneur, but I was blessed to have several amazing mentors throughout my formative years.

My first inspiration really came when I was in high school, and where I was starting to get into basketball a little bit. So to just have a positive, inspiring basketball coach, who was there at the time, who really saw the potential deep within me, well before I saw it, well before I realized it. But he saw something there. And I think that just encouraged me to keep on trying. Neither one of us knew how it would turn out, how good I would be, but we at least gave it a shot and kept on the track to keep on going.

Growing up, I was pretty introverted, pretty shy kind of kid, oversized, big, and tall, and uncoordinated. My coach could see that was who I was at that time as a high schooler. And I wasn't very athletic, so I had to just start from scratch. But he really took the time. He gave me my whole junior year in high school just to practice behind the scenes and to get familiar with the game of basketball. I never played a game in my junior year, but I practiced every single day with the team, without the team, kind of rounding in to become an athlete finally. And it took somebody like him to realize that's the kind of kid I was. If he pushed me too hard, I was probably going to quit and run away and not try. But he just created these little baby steps for me and encouraged me to keep on going. And it took a whole year of practice before I finally felt comfortable enough and confident enough to get out there and try to the game of basketball as a senior in high school.

In addition to encouraging me, he was also holding me accountable at the same time without being too overbearing. He didn't coddle me with kid gloves, but he encouraged me, and he kept on trying to help me to see that, "Hey, if I at least give it a try, who knows how good I might be?"

I was just an average player in high school, but at seven-feet tall, coaches start salivating over a kid that size. I got an athletic scholarship to Washington State University, and luckily, I was able to find another coach very similar to my high school coach who took his time with me, who gave me time to develop without bruising my confidence and having me quit the game. My freshman and sophomore years at Washington State, I hardly ever played a game. I'd sit the bench every game and maybe get in when the game was already decided one way or the other. He might throw me in there for the last minute or minute and a half or so. And that was it. So that's what I did my freshman and sophomore year at Washington State.

Well, I was practicing every day, even as a freshman and sophomore. I was in the weight room getting bigger and stronger and tougher and more athletic all the time. I was running stadium stairs. This was a complete makeover, a complete build of an athlete, and a student athlete at that. By the time I was a junior at Washington State, I had moved into the starting lineup. Some of the responsibility of making our team successful fell on me, and I rose to the challenge and met it head on. At that point, I started falling in love with the game of basketball. I didn't love this game the first two or three years, but at that point I fell in love with the game, and I just wanted to see how far I could take it.

The NBA years

I never thought about playing in the NBA until near my graduation as a senior from Washington State University. I started getting interest from different teams, but I wasn't good enough to make the NBA at that point, even though I got drafted by the Seattle SuperSonics in 1979. I chose to go overseas for one year and played in Italy for my first professional year where I could play the whole game. Only sitting on the Sonic's bench or somebody else's bench in the NBA, rarely getting a chance to play, my development would've really been stunted. But going to Italy, I was playing forty minutes a night, getting double points from rebounds, double figures in points. That's what made me the player I became because I was able to work on my skills and my game. I came back ready to go for the NBA the next year. It's the behind-the-scenes work that no one ever sees. They just look at the finished product and imagine that you've always been that way, but, no, I had a long way to go.

My first year with the Seattle SuperSonics, I started out as a backup center to Jack Sikma, who was the starting center at the time. I was actually the third center on the team behind Dennis Awtrey, also, so I rarely played the first half of my rookie season. I'd pop in again a minute or two here or there, but it really wasn't much to look at. And then when the backup center, Dennis Awtrey, got injured, that's when I started playing a lot more and really started making a lot of big contributions. It was an opportunity where I seized the opportunity and made something out of it.

During this time, I was focusing on just becoming an NBA player and being the best that I could be. I was surrounded by great leaders. I mean, Lenny Wilkens was the coach, and he's one of the greatest coaches and leaders I've ever had in my life. And this was an older veteran team that had just won the NBA World Championship the year before in 1979. They had a lot of established veteran players, who were providing the leadership to young guys like me, including Jack Sikma, Fred Brown, John Johnson, and guys who had been around for ten or more years in the NBA. I was just getting started, so I owe a big debt of gratitude and credit to so many of those guys who were patient with me and helped

me to develop at my own pace so I could contribute to the team quickly.

Next, I went to play with the San Diego Clippers, which turned into the LA Clippers the very next year. I was with the Clippers for three years. There, I became a full-time center in the starting lineup, playing every single game, putting up points and rebounds every night. Even though we had a bad team, and we didn't win often, I was able to develop a lot.

We didn't have the greatest coaches and the greatest team at that point, but those three years helped me to establish myself as an NBA player. One year, I won the field goal percentage, a championship leadership. I had the highest field goal percentage in the league, one of those years with the Los Angeles Clippers. I was becoming a good player, and that's when the Dallas Mavericks came calling.

I played seven years in Dallas. That was the pinnacle of my career, being around a lot of great players, All-Star players, guys like Rolando Blackman and Mark Aguirre, and a Hall of Fame coach in Dick Motta. We had a very good team in Dallas for several of those years. I made the NBA All-Star team in 1988, so this was really the apex of my career.

Midway through my last season in Dallas, I got traded to the New York Knicks and finished up with the New York Knicks in 1992. We had a very, very good team there as well, losing in the Eastern Conference Finals in the seventh game against Michael Jordan and the Bulls.

When I finally retired, I was ready. I retired after twenty professional seasons, including six of those seasons overseas, and I was forty-two years old, which was very old for an athlete. I had already created my pathway, my transition to what I was going to do next after sports, and that was to run my physical therapy business that I had established about ten years earlier.

The Donaldson Clinic

I was the image and the name of the Donaldson Clinic, and I was also the financier. I was the bank that invested my money into it to get it started. My NBA background helped me to see doctors and referring physicians all over the Seattle area. Having a name that was highly recognizable, especially back then, doctors were more than happy to stop everything and meet with me to understand what services we could provide. That was my main job for most of those years. I never was a physical therapist, although I went to school for my prerequisites.

We had multiple locations, so I spent a lot of time in the smaller satellite locations and was involved with the community, joining the various business networking groups, the chambers of commerce, the rotary club,

and neighborhood associations. I was very involved in all the different neighborhoods we were established in.

I think our biggest challenge was competing as a privately-owned business against the big corporations that were coming through and gobbling up many of the smaller, private, independent clinics. They had the ability to work on a scale of volume, providing deep discounts with the insurance companies. We weren't quite able to get to that level of growth to allow that, which was the biggest challenge throughout the twenty-eight years that we ran the business.

Another big challenge was being beholden to the insurance companies. The physical therapy business is a third-party payer kind of business, so we would provide the service, bill the insurance company, then wait to be reimbursed by them. Worse, they only pay for what they feel is fair. The margins just kept getting smaller, as the expenses went up. I think we closed at a really good time, 2018, especially before the pandemic, which would've really put a big crimp in everything.

Looking back, I don't think there's anything I would've done differently. I was a 100% owner so maybe bringing another partner on board or two to help share some of the liability costs would have helped. I took on all the liability on myself, so I was responsible for all the bills. Either the corporation could pay it, or I had to pay it personally. But I loved running the business. I loved being part of the community and giving back to the various communities.

We were in a couple of underserved communities in central Seattle and central Tacoma, which is about thirty miles south of Seattle. Those were my two favorite neighborhoods, and were historically Black neighborhoods, underserved, underdeveloped, and under-invested in. So we invested in them, and we hired from the community. I thought we did a great job. And you can't really do that when you have partners or investors who you are beholden to. The way I went about it gave me complete freedom to do exactly what I wanted to do. And the average small business goes in and out of business within two and a half years, but we hung around for twenty-eight years. It just ran its course, and it was time to move on.

Learning to pivot

After I retired at the age of 42, I was still in the gym five days a week, lifting weights, running two or three days a week, two or three miles at a time, and kept myself in excellent condition and shape. I never had any issue with my heart throughout all these years. And then when I got to be 57 years of age, I noticed I was starting to slow down a little bit. I was starting to get more fatigued. I couldn't run as easily as I used to. And I didn't really attribute that to anything. I just thought I was not in as great a shape as I used to be.

But on the morning of January 3, 2015, I was out getting ready to play a round of golf with my buddies. We had not even teed off yet off. I said, "Guys, I just don't feel too well today. My back is killing me. I'm already sweating profusely. We haven't even swung to clubs yet." I was feeling nauseous. I said, "I think I'm just going to go

and see my doctor. I going to see if I can get in and see him real quick."

I left the golf game and drove myself twenty minutes to the doctor's office. I vaguely remember seeing the reception counter of the lobby in his office, and then everything went black at that point.

The doctor later told me they had done a quick diagnostic scan, determined it was my heart, threw me into the ambulance, and then straight into surgery for a twelve-hour open-heart emergency surgery on an aortic dissection. I woke up two weeks later.

Of course, with a major invasive surgery like that, there are always complications. We had to do a follow-up surgery the next year and then another follow-up surgery in 2018, and yet another follow-up surgery in 2020. Within five years, I had four major surgeries.

During this time, I couldn't focus on my business anymore. I was in pain, and I was on medication. My business was being run very well with the management team I had in place. But they're managers. They're not the decision makers. They're not the drivers of somebody who owns the business.

Before you know it, we had lost our steam. We had lost our momentum. And we started having financial challenges that I was trying to resolve by spending my own money to save it, hundreds and hundreds of thousands of dollars. I exhausted all my NBA savings, thinking I was going to be able to pull it out, but I couldn't. We had to close the doors in February 2018.

I'll never forget the day I had to call the whole staff in on a Monday morning, and instead of opening for business as we usually do, I had to tell they we were out of business. They had to clean out their lockers and pick up their last paycheck. It was the hardest thing I've ever had to do.

That's probably why I spent my life savings because I felt terribly obligated to twenty-five employees to keep going as long as we could. In 2018, the banks still weren't financing small businesses like ours, especially if you had some financial challenges. The banks weren't taking the risks that they used to take ten years previously.

Back in the recession of 2008, we had to close two or three of our locations because they just weren't cash-flowing positively. And the banks had dried up all the money, so you couldn't borrow any more. We managed to hang on another ten years after that, but each year, the margins became smaller, and the expenses became greater. The handwriting was on the wall, but I wanted to hang in there as long as I possibly could.

Coming back from a dark year

After my emergency open-heart surgery, I entered a dark time. My mother died and then my wife walked out on our marriage of many years, taking my stepson with her. I wasn't able to focus on the business anymore, and after using up my life savings to keep it afloat, we finally had to close the Donaldson Clinic down. I also lost my home that I had lived in for forty years. Everything fell apart.

During this time, I slipped into a deep depression along with anxiety and suicidal ideations. I had lost my business, my life savings, my marriage, my mother, and my health. All I had left was my life, which I was threatening to take at any moment. It was pure hell and darkness that I wouldn't wish on my worst enemy.

I realized to help me get back on my feet mentally and emotionally, I needed to regain my purpose. I had totally lost my purpose in life because I was no longer a business owner, no longer a husband, no longer in good health, and no longer financially stable. But once the darkness started lifting, I realized, after many conversations with God, that I still had a platform and a voice. People could hear my story, and they could resonate with what I went through. And that's when I started up Your Gift of Life Foundation.

Your Gift of Life Foundation

Currently, the foundation is a resource hub for everything related to mental health. On the website there are a whole list of helpful resources. My story is on there, plus there are ways for them to get a hold of me. And many of them do.

I feel driven to help people who suffer the same pain I did. There are 132 suicides every day, 22 of them are by veterans, many of them homeless. I have a platform and a voice, and I use it to help people who are suffering from all mental challenges, not just suicide.

There are many different aspects to what the foundation does. It essentially gives me a platform to go out and do a lot of

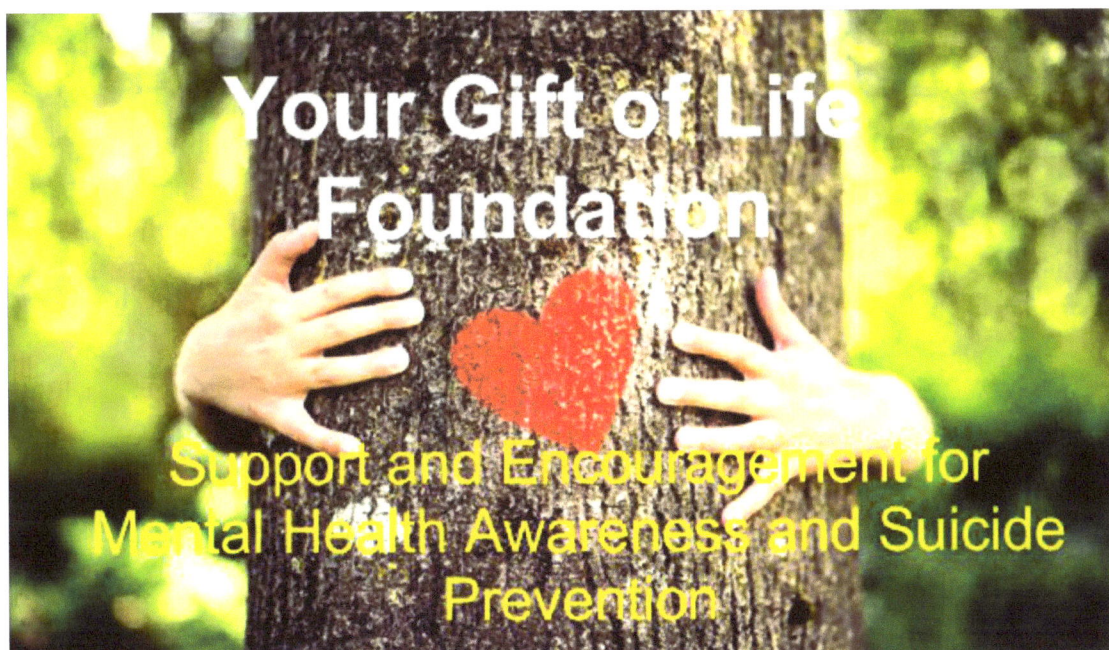

Your Gift of Life Foundation

Support and Encouragement for Mental Health Awareness and Suicide Prevention

speaking engagements, which I love to do. Everything dried up the last couple of years because of COVID, but I love speaking to our young people. I love speaking to military groups, men, business groups—you name it. I love helping others. This fall, when school's back in session, I hope to be able to hit the road and travel to speaking engagements all over the country.

I also began writing my book, *Celebrating Your Gift of Life: From the Verge of Suicide to a Life of Purpose and Joy*, shortly after starting up the foundation. I thought, *I have to put this on paper. I have to chronicle what I went through for those twelve dark months and let people know there is hope. There's light at the end of the tunnel. You have to keep on plugging away.* My book has a lot of helpful strategies and suggestions that I utilize that will be very helpful for everybody else.

This is actually my second book. I wrote another book about ten years ago called *Standing Above the Crowd*. It's more of an inspirational and motivational book, while *Celebrating Your Gift of Life* is more of a self-help book.

Entrepreneurship

I was first exposed to business while attending Washington State University and then while learning how to invest the money I earned while playing in the NBA. Tax shelters were all the rage back then, and I learned how to invest in real estate, business opportunities, and most traditional investment vehicles.

However, I truly became an entrepreneur when I started the Donaldson Clinic while playing for the Dallas Mavericks. I went from investing in businesses to owning one. We had several locations and a staff of twenty-five to thirty people. I continued to play professional basketball another ten years while running that business, which lasted twenty-eight years altogether.

During those first ten years, I would come home during the off season and engage fully in the business. I took classes to become a physical therapist so I could understand the business from a hands-on perspective. I learned how all aspects of the business worked from physical therapy to massage therapy to finances to billing and working with insurance companies and banks. It was important that it wasn't just my name on the business but that I also knew it intimately.

My father was a twenty-year veteran of the United States Air Force, so I witnessed the similarities between the military and professional sports. Both provide valuable experience and lessons that help you to be successful in business. My father was strict and lived a very disciplined life. He was always in tip-top shape, even as he grew older. That example instilled in me how to be persistent and successful.

To be successful in sports, just as in business, you learn how to work hard as a team and how to work together toward a common goal or vision. You learn the value of persistence and never giving up. You have good days and bad days, but you keep plugging away with your eye on the prize. You never win every game, so you examine your losses and create a new game plan and then go at it just as hard the next day. You never give up.

In the military, you also learn how to lead a team of high performers. Like participating in athletics, serving in the military teaches you leadership. You learn discipline and how to follow orders or direction. You learn how to lead by example. You learn how to *be* the example for those you are leading.

If you have a chance to play team sports or join the military, I highly recommend you take it. These are two of the best personal development programs out there, especially for achieving high levels of business success.

Learn more about James Donaldson and the Your Gift of Life Foundation at yourgiftoflife.org.

Going Rogue

The Directors of Rogue Publishing Partners

Shelby Jo Long, Director and CEO

As a professor, I have been around the publishing industry with writing, editing, and publishing in academic journals for fifteen years. As an entrepreneur, I have worked on the business side of the publishing industry for the past two years. I help authors transform their book into a high-ticket coaching program or course.

It often seems to be a challenge for authors to see the opportunities for their ideas within their books and to look at their writing in terms of its potential for other income streams. The first challenge is getting your ideas in your book. The second challenge is thinking about other ways you can use the content and information to create new and different income streams for your business. I help clients find ways to make a greater impact with their audiences and turn their ideas into dollars.

I've learned that your professional network is your net worth. When you surround yourself with supportive partners, you expand your level of influence in the marketplace. And when the partners in your network share your business with their networks, and those people share it with their networks—your influence (and eventually, your income) becomes unlimited.

Susie Schaefer, Director and VP of Publishing and Operations

I started in the publishing industry in 2016, right after my divorce, when I wasn't sure what the path was for my life. A dear friend of mine introduced me to independent publishing and took me under her wing, where I learned everything there is to know about the publishing industry, and began working as a certified publishing consultant, building a client roster with like-minded souls, and giving them the opportunity to be proud of their accomplishments as authors.

A few years later, when I moved back to California to be closer to family, it became apparent that it was time for me to spread my wings and launch my own business. Thus, the birth of the pineapple logo, a nod to my background in the hospitality industry and the epitome of welcoming and friendship, something I value in working with my clients.

As a child, I was an avid reader, and loved the feel of a fabric cover and the smell of a library. Those childhood memories stem from my mother reading to me every day, instilling in me a deep sense of the importance of books in our lives. Today, I continue to read as a hybrid reader, through physical books, on my e-reader, and listening to audiobooks when my eyes need to rest.

I believe in the written word, the sharing of stories, and I stand up to censorship, something we're witnessing in today's world. My mission is to empower authors to share their story with the world and give the gift of themselves in their published work.

Writing a book is no small feat, and I commend those that embark on the journey of writing. Many of the authors I work with are sharing themselves, and sometimes that comes with unhealed trauma, a sense of unworthiness, or simply not feeling confident. It's my job to unwrap those emotions and provide them support, encouragement, and holding a safe space for them to share.

My favorite books to work on are those that are part business, part memoir. I like to pride myself with empowering authors to share a piece of themselves by bringing together what I call "The Trifecta" – their story, their brand, and their community to connect their mission and their message and create a ripple effect of social impact through "cause" publishing.

The greatest lesson I've learned is to embrace my spiritual gifts and use them in my business. As an intuitive with clairsentient/claircognizant abilities, I needed to share those gifts when working with my clients. The magic happens when we discover how to "connect the dots" so that they come away from the experience of writing and publishing with a renewed sense of excitement for their business and have the confidence to share themselves with their own audience. This creates deeper relationships, more trust, and garners clients that are more in alignment with their business values.

Chris O'Byrne, Director and VP of Publishing

I've been in the publishing industry for around 15 years. It wasn't inspiration as much as dumb luck that got me into publishing. I started out in the Air Force, became a chemical engineer, pivoted into teaching high school, then eventually became determined to start my own business. I had stumbled into freelance editing and one day one of my authors asked if I knew how to make an ebook. I said sure, went online to learn how, and then turned her short manuscript into an ebook. The same thing happened with covers and print interiors, and I finally realized I had my business.

The biggest challenge I've seen is an unwillingness to pay for good service. An author will put an unbelievable number of hours into their manuscript and then

lose all momentum near the end. I've seen authors insist they don't need an edit (they do) and that they can do the design themselves (they can't). Failing to pay for good editing results in the complete failure of a book. And failing to have great design done results in an unprofessional presentation and fewer sales.

The great lesson I've learned is that I'm not nearly as smart of a businessman as I've duped myself into believing all these years. For a long time, I thought I was very smart and that I could do everything on my own. One day, I challenged myself to be completely honest about myself. That was eye-opening and painful. But, the end result was that I made some incredible partnerships that have made everything in my business life much better. I don't need to be a super-smart businessman when I have a whole team of smart businesspeople surrounding me. And doing everything on my own was miserable, anyway.

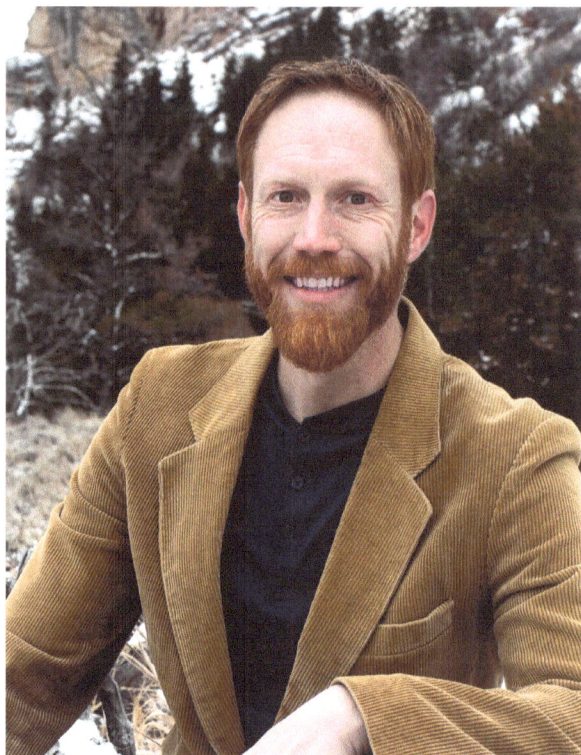

Scott Sery, Director and VP of Badassery

My role is to create stories that inspire, draw people in, and intrigue. I suppose it started in college when I had to write hundreds of essays each semester. As an anthropology and sociology major, I was tasked with taking difficult, dense, and often archaic texts, analyzing them, and turning them into a coherent collection of words that anyone could understand.

That transformed into a writing career many years later. I had the background and the skill and discovered that writing provided much more joy than just about

any other "job" out there. Now, fourteen-ish years later, I'm still writing.

Most people are really bad at writing. I'm not condemning them; that's just the way it is. They took a few English classes through their schooling but never pursued it much beyond that. There really was no reason to keep going with it. As they see more and more success with their businesses, they realize they have a cool story … that they have no idea how to tell.

I work with them to pull the juicy details out of the story, turn it into a magnificent, published piece and help them show off what they're all about.

Don't be too quiet. In person, I'm quiet and reserved and prefer to observe rather than talk. When it comes to your business, no matter if you're a writer, a business owner, or a professional, don't be scared to share what you do and why you're the most amazing at it ever.

Clamming up because you don't want to annoy people leads to people not knowing what you do. When people don't know what you do, they aren't able to refer business to you, and you end up struggling far more than necessary. Tell everyone what you do and why you do it and tell them often.

Jennifer Jas, Director and VP of Editing

I've always loved words, and I'm honored to spend my work hours with my hands, head, and heart immersed in helping people share their words in brilliant ways. My book-editing journey began in the early 2000s when I helped create a book for a friend who had served as a Merchant Marine in

World War II. That first book lit a fire in my soul, and for the next fifteen years, I edited books as a side gig while working as a writer, spokesperson, and manager in corporate communications for the health care and manufacturing industries.

In 2017, I finally made the leap to full-time editing when I launched Words With Jas, a nonfiction editing service. For a person who loves to read, I'm lucky to get to read all day as I help writers create engaging, well-written, and accurate books and digital content.

One challenge writers often face is that they wonder if their writing is any good. Sometimes, that thought alone is enough to cause writers to fear the blank screen or paper, avoid setting aside regular times to write, and procrastinate (maybe even for years!). But when they believe they have valuable ideas that people need to hear, and they understand that once they write their words, an editor can polish them, then it empowers them to write. More people would call themselves authors if they realized how much an experienced editor could turn their words into an excellent experience for the reader (and the author).

Another challenge new authors face is that they don't realize they need a team of experts to help them create and publish a quality book. They may have heard or assumed that they can DIY the book-publishing process, but they end up worn out and disappointed with the results and the reader reviews. It can be challenging for them to shift their thinking and realize that if it's important to them and their name will be on the front—they need to invest

in doing it right. And that involves hiring professionals for each part of the project.

I perform the editing role, and depending on the author's needs, I can connect them to experts who offer book visioning, coaching, formatting and design, marketing and PR, and branding. I'm thrilled to be a part of Rogue Publishing Partners, which offers custom solutions to help nonfiction authors choose their professionals to create the best books possible.

I spent my early years as an editor saying "yes" way too often. This practice led me to work long hours, usually seven days a week, and sacrifice time for myself and my family and friends. It also created a lack of time for strategic and creative thinking. I've since learned to share a clear message about the types of clients and projects I attract and only say "yes" to those projects that are a good fit for my expertise and interests. Then I can give those clients my best while thriving personally and professionally.

Michelle White, Director and VP of Design

I started out in general print design and later transitioned to designing textbooks. I started my design business over twenty years ago. As an avid reader and lover of learning with experience in textbook design, I made the natural decision to focus on nonfiction books. I am grateful to have worked with so many interesting topics and wonderful authors over the years, and I've never looked back.

The biggest challenge for authors is to articulate what they like and don't like in terms of visual representation of their books. It's hard for many people to visualize how a concept will look on a book cover or in the interior pages. I love to distill the essence of their book into the perfect combination of image, type, and color that not only appeals to them, but also attracts readers too.

Self-publishing authors also face challenges in planning, editing, distribution, and marketing, which is why I've teamed up with Rogue Publishing Partners. I now have a network of other professionals to help my clients with all aspects of getting a successful book out there.

I've learned that the most important aspect of any transaction is communication. Making sure the client and I are on the same page sets expectations at the start and prevents misunderstandings later on, and when conflict does arise, good communication is essential in finding mutually agreeable solutions. Also, clear explanations of my design choices help clients to see their book within the larger context of the marketplace.

Jason Miller, Principal Chairman

I have zero experience in the publishing industry. My main focus is business growth and scale for companies. I created the Rogue Publishing Partners model to assist with the development, growth, and scale of several clients who are in the publishing industry.

I see business leaders who want to write books to show their expertise and provide valuable information and knowledge, yet they don't know exactly what to write about or the steps they should take. They need help with the publishing process. Also, many authors find it challenging to share their books in strategic ways once the books are completed and published. So many books are published and then go nowhere because the authors did nothing with the opportunity.

Speed loves money, and money loves speed. Move fast, implement strategy, and pivot and micro-pivot very quickly to adapt to your marketplace.

The Rogue Publishing Partners story

A group of seven founding members have created a groundbreaking consortium specifically designed for nonfiction authors. Featuring professional publishing and business services, the Rogue Publishing Partners platform offers a host of experts in the independent publishing industry to help executives, entrepreneurs, coaches, and consultants write, publish, and market books designed to give them traction in the marketplace.

Studies show that being a published author can help professionals get the recognition they deserve and provide the path for increasing profits and gaining more clients. Rogue Publishing Partners can help them take control of the self-publishing process.

The experience of publishing a book can be life changing. After an author has spent so much time and effort on creating their manuscript, their finished book should look like it was produced by a big New York publishing house. Unfortunately, too many self-published authors fall short of this goal by cutting corners and skipping critical steps, ultimately putting out unprofessional books that undercut their message.

At RoguePublishingPartners.com, authors can choose specific services or work with a publishing expert to create professional books that speak to their mission and message. From ghostwriting, editing, and book design, to marketing, PR, and program development, Rogue Publishing Partners has all the necessary resources in one place.

In collaboration with the Strategic Advisor Board, Rogue Publishing Partners was developed as a side-by-side platform to support the community of professional service providers and their clients. Our mission is to assist executives, coaches, consultants, and entrepreneurs who want to write and publish nonfiction books to amplify their message, further their mission, and build community around their area of expertise.

Beyond the Song and Dance of Personal Branding

Phillip Lanos

Going viral

When it comes to personal branding for business leaders, going viral is at the front of the line and the "lowest hanging fruit" target for CEOs.

Manufacturing the right mix of timing and relevancy is rarely something one person or even a team can do. All you have to do is read Malcom Gladwell's book *Tipping Point* or *Contagious* by Jonah Berger to begin your journey of understanding how much trial and error, along with luck, play a role in this endeavor.

Anything left up to chance is what I like to call "hope marketing" and that isn't going to do much for your personal brand, especially if you have none to begin with. That's why understanding who you are and who you're trying to reach is so empowering in the building of a personal brand.

You stand to have much more control by creating a strategy and executing with consistency. The biggest challenge is how a CEO makes time to focus on this while running a business.

If you have trouble making time for the development of your personal brand as a CEO, you don't have a time problem, you have a business problem.

If you're the bottleneck that your business has to run through to operate, that's an entirely different set of issues you're facing.

Clarity of message

Once you've committed to the idea of investing into the development of your personal brand as a CEO, it's time to get your message in order.

Whatever you do, do not make it sound like a business website's copy that is often vague and filled with business jargon. Make the effort to humanize your language and use "it's" instead of "it is." Use more contractions in your message. It's more conversational and a master principle of writing copy.

To build a solid message, you'll need:

1. A targeted audience who'll receive your message
2. A promise to that audience
3. Reasons why they should believe you
4. How their life will be better because they've met you or will stay in touch with you

I've oversimplified what I'm sharing here, but without all four, your efforts are going to fail no matter the size of your budget.

As Seth Godin says in his book *All Marketers Are Liars*, "Good Marketing only helps bad products fail faster." Be sure to invest in the crafting of your message.

One last note, please invest in some decent headshots with different looks. One business, one casual, and one everyday look related to something personal like a hiking outfit or t-shirt from your favorite band. If you don't have these assets, you should make getting them a priority. Good pictures can be used for years so divide the expense of them in that way.

Management of your online presence

Once you've prepared your message, it's time to decide what channels are relevant and where you should spend your time managing your online presence. Not everyone needs to be on Facebook or LinkedIn. It depends on what you're doing and who you're trying to reach.

This also means that Forbes, Entrepreneur, or Inc. should be scrutinized for relevancy. The brand power and name don't mean a thing if you can't justify that your target spends time consuming content there.

Although creating content and assets like a book or course are important, there's more to it. Part of personal branding means you invest time connecting and speaking to people online without trying to sell anything.

This means taking the time to build connections and learn about others in the community you're trying to be part of, not just leveraging or using them. This level of integrity to your approach will make the entire journey of building your brand align with your highest ideals.

> *There has never been a better time to have a personal brand with social media as active as it is now, and 100 followers is enough if they're targeted and qualified followers. If you stay away from vanity metrics, you win more in both the short-term and long-term, but this kind of winning requires a clear understanding and documented personal brand.*
>
> **– Phillip Lanos**

Does this mean you can't assign an assistant to manage your personal brand? No, but it's *how*, not *what*.

If you have your personal assistant helping, they should not be tasked with creating the responses. But they can be asked to collect the most relevant and important questions or comments you're receiving and bring them to your attention in a curated manner to save you time.

You can tell them how you want to respond, and your assistant should know about the message you crafted and all four of its parts so that they can correct you if one of your responses is not aligned with your personal brand message.

There are also many online tools that can be leveraged to help collect data and automate repetitive tasks, but you should strive to manage your online brand with as much of a personal touch as you can afford to. Otherwise, you run the risk of being out of touch.

Phillip Lanos has interviewed over 1,000 CEOs while host of both the Entrepreneur and Inc. magazine podcasts. He also helped launch podcasts for Entrepreneur Organization also known as EO, a global network of entrepreneurs. Phillip owns Own The Rhythm, a personal branding agency that helps entrepreneurs clarify their online messaging and develop a strategy for communications across social media and everywhere online.

The Business of CBD

Melanie Kossan

When I first began working with CBD, people in my area either didn't know what it was, or they had serious misconceptions about it. It would have been easy to say, "This market is not going to work for CBD," but instead, I launched into education.

I created and taught CBD School, went on the largest radio station in the area every month to talk about CBD and answer questions from listeners, plus ran informational ads on television. It went a long way to create a marketing path for the product.

More recently, my main competition has been the reputations of other CBD sellers. There are some companies out there providing high-quality products, but it is a lot easier to find someone who is selling cooking oil and calling it CBD oil. There are also oils out there that contain very few cannabinoids, so when someone does decide to try it out, it doesn't work. This has created distrust and skepticism in consumers.

Millions of Americans use CBD daily and love it. However, depending on how it is produced and the actual amount of cannabinoids in the product, your results may vary.

I have personally developed the recipes for every product we offer. I have sourced our cannabinoid ingredients from Mountain Meadow CBD, a Montana farm with whom we've developed a dynamic working relationship. Bryan Bennett of Mountain Meadow CBD was recently on my podcast, *Who's Your Mama?* and said:

"I recommend everyone go look at stillwaterhemp.com, see what she has to offer. My products are very basic, and Mountain Mama's products are a bit more sophisticated. I'm very happy that we were able to meet and be a part of this and that we can offer Montana-grown CBD through your Montana-owned company."

Due to a variety of physical ailments, a high percentage of regular users count on CBD to enable them to enjoy the best possible quality of life. Studies have shown that most CBD users are seeking to address specific conditions, making it much more than a faddish supplement.

Over the past several years, clinical studies by reputable researchers have found CBD can be effective in treating chronic pain, anxiety, inflammation, migraine, insomnia, PTSD, fibromyalgia, multiple sclerosis (MS), muscular dystrophy, and a variety of other complaints.

Unfortunately, the old adage, "buyer beware," applies to every purchase you make as a cannabidiol consumer. As the founder of a CBD business in Montana, I knew from the get-go that the quality and purity of my offerings would be key to winning the loyalty of customers.

Equally important was to provide peace of mind through total transparency of where I source the hemp and how it is processed, and by stating the precise dosage of cannabinoids on my labeling to ensure responsible use and maximum efficacy.

Before spending your hard-earned money, I suggest using these pointers to be sure what you buy measures up to the standards you expect and deserve:

7 Items you should check before buying another CBD product

1. Is it whole plant?

The best CBD oil is extracted from the leaves, flowers, and stalks of the hemp plant, not just one portion of the plant. Be sure that the product you are buying comes from a whole-plant extract. There is no getting around the fact that the best way to get all the most useful cannabinoids out of a hemp plant is to distill the entire plant.

2. Avoid hemp seed oil products

Read the label. If it says hemp seed oil it will be extremely low in cannabinoids. CBD is one of over 100 cannabinoids in the hemp plant. Again, real CBD oil is extracted from the hemp plant. In contrast, hemp oil is made by cold pressing the seeds only. Therefore, it has almost no properties that

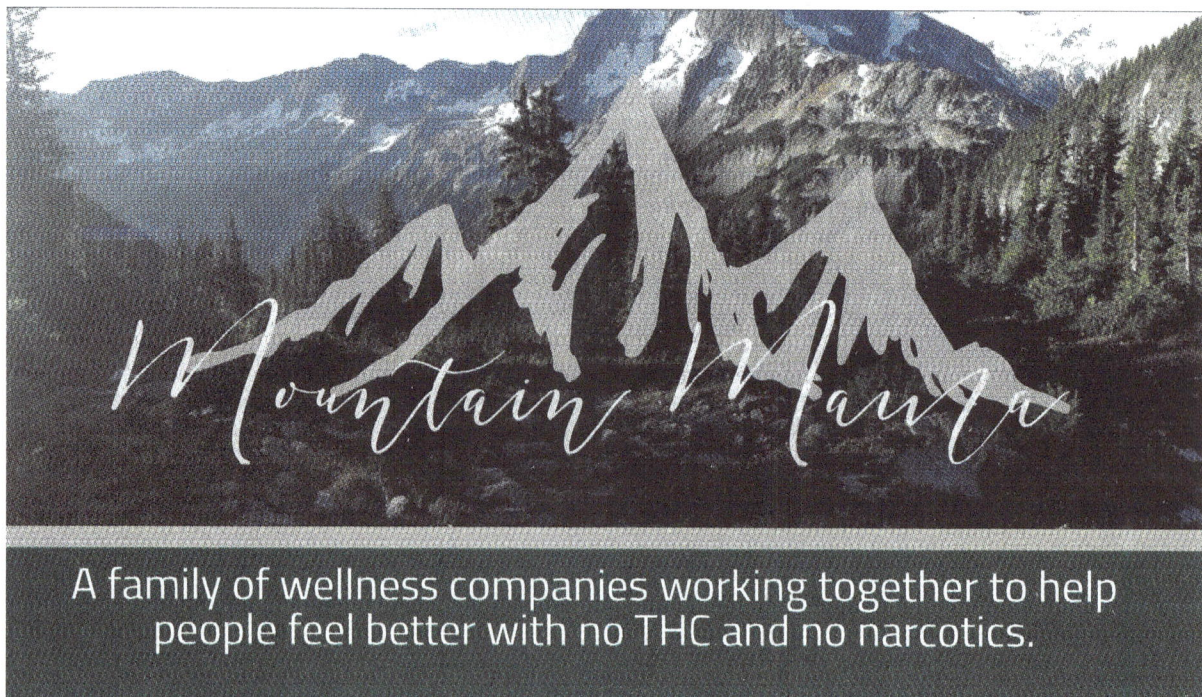

A family of wellness companies working together to help people feel better with no THC and no narcotics.

affect the human cannabinoid system. Hemp seed oil is rich in linoleic acid and can be used as cooking oil. Linoleic acid has been shown to reduce total cholesterol and low-density lipoprotein, also known as "bad" cholesterol. It may also be useful as a treatment of acne. A quality CBD product will say on the label how many milligrams of CBD is in the product.

3. Is a laboratory Certificate of Analysis (COA) available?

Make sure that the product you are buying provides a hyperlink or printed Certificate of Analysis. This means that it has been tested by a third-party laboratory to confirm the level of cannabinoids (also referred to as potency) in the product. It will also tell you if there are impurities such as heavy metals, pesticides, herbicides, and other chemicals or compounds that may not be desirable. My COAs are on my website. I've also gone the extra mile to create a QR Code that links to my COAs, and it is on every product we make.

4. Is the CBD from oil or isolate?

Be sure there are multiple cannabinoids in the product you're using. A topical product may contain only CBD or CBD isolate and still be effective. However, any product you are taking internally such as a tincture or an edible should have multiple cannabinoids in it to be beneficial. You will see this referred to as the "entourage effect," When a wide spectrum of cannabinoids works together, they create what is called "homeostasis," or the physiological process used to maintain a healthy equilibrium in the endocannabinoid system and is key to the healthy functioning of our bodies.

The endocannabinoid system (ECS) found in all mammals and invertebrates is a cell-signaling system responsible for regulating a wide spectrum of physiological functions, including sleep, pain, digestion, immune response, etc. Two of the three components of the ECS are cannabinoid receptors (CB1 and CB2) mostly located in the central nervous system and immune system. The other element of ECS relevant to the use of CBD are endocannabinoids, which are cannabinoids naturally produced within the human body. If you are using an ingestible CBD product that has a poor-quality CBD not sourced from the whole plant, you will not benefit from the entourage effect.

5. How was it processed?

Make sure you are buying CBD from a vertically integrated manufacturer. For example, Stillwater Hemp products are all made in-house. We source our distillates from a Montana hemp farm which meets the FDA's guidelines as an organic grower. The most common ways to extract cannabinoids from the hemp plant are:

1. Carbon dioxide extraction pumps CO_2 into pressurized chambers, creating high pressure and low temperatures to produce hemp oil high in CBD. Safe and effective, this method also leaves no toxic residue whatsoever.
2. Steam distillation uses a distillation tank filled with heated water, pushing steam to another tank containing the plant, which results in oil vapors containing CBD.
3. Solvent extraction works much like steam distillation but uses a solvent instead of water. Due to the use

of flammable compounds such as butane, propane, or ethanol, this method can be hazardous and has the potential to leave toxins in the final product. All Stillwater Hemp products are processed using CO_2 or steam methods.

6. Is the hemp organic and non-GMO?

As with anything you put into your body, natural and pure choices are best. The best quality CBD products are whole plant, grown without the use of pesticides, insecticides, herbicides, or genetically modified seeds, and naturally processed without chemicals. As part of our commitment to oversight of our supply chain, we meet frequently with the owner of the FDA-certified organic farm where all our hemp is grown. Many CBD products use isolates or CBD oil sourced from another distributor and are simply slapping their own label on it. Knowing how your CBD products of choice are produced is the best way to ensure quality and efficacy.

7. Does the label include the legally required information?

Read the label carefully. The label should contain at least three items: the name of the producer, a detailed list of ingredients, and how many milligrams of CBD are in the product. These are the basic three facts that you need to know to be assured that you are getting good value and the potency you expect. Labeling laws differ from state to state, so there may be additional information offered by the manufacturer and required to meet those laws. In many states, a telephone number and the street address of the producer is mandatory.

I hope this checklist is helpful to you as a user of CBD in its many forms. Despite the problems inherent in the consumer products sector of the hemp industry, I am a firm believer that CBD is here to stay. In just the past few years, especially since the passing of the 2018 Farm Bill, the CBD industry has come a long way. Formal recognition of the value of the naturally occurring compounds in the Cannabis Sativa L. plant by virtually all states paves the way for further research and continued innovation by producers.

Melanie Kossan is the founder of Mountain Mama, LLC, a Montana-based Organic health and CBD company. The company now fulfills ecommerce orders across all fifty states and private label orders for other businesses selling CBD products.

Live with Intention to Pursue Your Purpose

Otis McGregor

Tribe + Purpose (Tribe and Purpose) was founded to help people pursue their purpose while living their life with intention. We also realize that no one does it alone, and that is why we added tribe to our name.

Business owners go through many stages in their businesses' successes and failures. These stages depend on the business owner and their perception of what is next and how they see things.

We've found that business owners who are veterans have a unique outlook on their business and their team. Many veterans start their businesses because they want the independence they never had while serving. The irony is that most business owners spend more time on their company than they did when they were in the military.

This is because veterans are problem solvers. Sure, they all know how to delegate. That is a fundamental leadership skill taught in every service. But something changes when the veteran starts his own business—they forget those fundamentals of delegation.

Or, just as likely, they are so emotionally attached to the business that they think they are the only ones who can do it. The emotional attachment is what does every one of them in, then they hit burnout and frustration.

Their frustrations lead to burnout and will eventually kill the business. The veteran business owner knows how to hide it from the team, but the team senses something. Only the seasoned team members understand what is going on and see it no matter how well the owner tries to hide it.

Now, the revenue is plateauing or falling, but the key team members are also developing doubts about their job security and the company's health. They start to talk at the coffee pot, or to use the old-school phrase, the water cooler, about what is going on in the company and whether or not it makes sense for them to stick around.

Guess what happens next? The business falters more, and now the owner feels even more pressure. It's proposal season. There's a recompete for one of the three major contracts that have sustained the business for the last four years.

Those members who were the experts in proposal writing are now looking at other companies. The team starts to divide and take on an attitude of *I have to save my job!* Or even worse, *I have to find another job quickly.* These people will jump to another company for a measly $2,000 more in annual salary or less.

How do you stop the bleeding?

You have to pause because nothing will get fixed if you keep running around trying to fix everything. Pause, and take an assessment of where you are. Where the business is, in other words.

It's time for a map check, and if you aren't sure where and who you are, it's time to find a known point so you can reference yourself and replot your course. Wandering around in circles in the woods will get you nowhere.

When you take the pause, you can identify what's important and what truly must be done to "right the course." This will allow you to truly see what needs to happen next, which fire is burning hot and close, so you can put it out and make another day, another week, another pay period.

Now the good work starts, and it's time to realign your vision with your company's movement. In other words, it's time to get your company back on azimuth to the outcome you originally set before everything drifted off course.

The next step is to determine where you want to be and where you want your business to be. We use a process called the

Ideal Day. This is the fun part because you get to be creative and create the ideal day for yourself five years from today.

Don't be general. Be specific with everything you want to do that day, from when you wake up in the morning to when you go to bed. The more details, the better.

For example, at 8:23 a.m., I drive 24 min to the office. While I'm driving, I listen to the Tim Ferris podcast, and so on for the entire day.

You will be amazed at what falls out for you. This will help you understand who and where you want to be in five years.

Now we can create a plan. You know where you are; you know where you want to be; let's connect the dots with the plan. This is your plan, not the plan for the business. We have to know who we are and where we want to go before we can lead anyone anywhere.

You now know where and who you want to be in five years and how your business fits into that plan. What does the business need to look like for you to achieve your personal outcome?

This plan is about guiding your business. As the owner, you are responsible for setting the model for what you want the vision to be. It's time to include your team in developing the plan.

Don't write your plan in the office and come out on the shop floor, drop it on the table, and tell them to go. That never works. The team must have buy-in, and the best way to get buy-in is to include your team in the planning.

Assign them sections to work on and develop. Give them ownership of creating and executing the plan. The ones who participate and buy-in are the ones who will be there when you hit the five-year outcome at three years.

In the midst of all these actions, you are part of the Tribe + Purpose's Power Tribe. The Power Tribe is a small group of business leaders who become your go-to tribe to exchange ideas, support each other's success, and, most importantly, help each member when they are down. You are not in this alone. The Power Tribe is your go-to resource for following through and both dealing with problems and celebrating success.

If you want to make a lot of money, you should go it alone—and you'll be very lonely at the top. If you're going to be successful, you need a tribe supporting you—and it'll never get lonely, no matter how high you climb.

Figure 2 Your Road Map to pursue your purpose and live life with intention

LTC, Special Forces, US Army, Retired Otis McGregor leads Tribe and Purpose with his son Camden. With over 40 years of experience as a leader, coach, and team member, Otis embodies the values and principles of Tribe and Purpose. He has empowered hundreds of businesses and individuals to find their clarity for purpose and their tribes for connection. Otis leverages the unique blend of heart, passion, and experience as one of the elite commanders of Green Berets.

Business Insights into the LLC

Julia Greenberg-Aguilar and Katerina Zuniga

Three common myths about registering your business

When it comes to forming an LLC or corporation, understanding the steps of registering your business is a critical component of the overall process. However, there are many misconceptions people believe when registering their businesses that cause them to make mistakes and hurt their business. Here are just a few of the most common myths about registering your business to help you navigate through the process as efficiently as possible.

Once your business is registered, nobody else can use your business name

Many people seem to take this myth as fact, and even though it may seem logical, it's not quite that simple in reality. The truth is that even though one of the benefits of an LLC includes the right to claim your business name, it only applies to businesses that are registered in the same state. It doesn't protect the same name from being used nationwide — you'd have to form your LLC in all 50 states to achieve that kind of individuality.

It's always wiser financially to start your LLC in a state without income tax

Of course, nobody enjoys paying taxes, but the fact is, this isn't always a better decision. States like Wyoming, Texas, South Dakota, and Nevada don't have income taxes, but again, it's not as simple as it sounds. The tax laws of your business come from the state that it's actually operated in.

"If you live in California, run your business from California, and make money in California, you most likely will be subject to paying California state taxes – even if you registered the business in Nevada," explains SecretEntourage.

Keep in mind that when considering an LLC vs corporation, this rule still applies.

Once you've completed the process of registering your business, you're done

In 2010, there were 27.9 million small businesses in the United States, and many of them would probably like to believe this is true. However, in addition to registering your business, there are further compliance requirements that must be met. These typically include filing an annual report and paying a small annual fee. There are different compliance requirements depending on whether you're forming an LLC vs corporation, so make sure you're aware and can keep up with the demands.

Ultimately, knowing the truth behind these myths can help you navigate through the business registration process as efficiently as possible. Don't let misconceptions get the best of your next venture.

The surprising tax advantages of starting an LLC

Setting up your own business can be overwhelming, but it may seem that much more challenging when you have to choose from the various forms of business models. Of course, a corporation and a limited liability company aren't really business models.

An LLC, or limited liability company, is often considered to be an especially beneficial form of business for a startup company. These types of businesses are easier to set up. But what is an LLC and what are the tax advantages of choosing this option?

What is an LLC?

Depending on the number of owners, the IRS automatically sees an LLC as a "disregarded entity" or partnership. This kind of business structure brings the limited liability of the company's owners together in much the same way a corporation would have, with that of the pass-through taxation that a partnership would have. LLC advantages in this area involve minimal taxes with generous legal protection.

LLC advantages with taxes

LLC advantages involving taxes include only filing for taxes once, reduced tax rates, and no double taxation. An LLC is only taxed once regardless of the number of owners. The net income of the business is taxed via a single owner of the company and in some cases the owner can file taxes for the business through their own personal tax return.

Depending on the total income of the LLC and the owner, the tax rates of the company may be lower than that of a corporation. This is because an LLC's tax rate is typically figured according to the personal tax rate of the owner. A personal tax rate is often reduced significantly in comparison to that of a corporate tax rate.

In addition to the LLC benefits of reduced tax rates, an LLC doesn't have to pay a double taxation as a corporate owner does. Corporate owners pay taxes on their dividend income as well as their corporate net income. An LLC on the other hand does not have to do this.

It should be noted that laws regarding the taxation of LLC varies from state and state. What one state does not require an LLC or corporation to pay may be required by another. If you are considering forming an LLC or have questions regarding the benefits of an LLC, be sure to check with the state law requirements for this business option before making a decision.

How small businesses can be either LLCs or corporations

American business entities can have one of many different types of legal structures.

The size of one's company does not define the type of legal structure chosen by the business owner. For instance, there were 27.9 million small business in the United States in 2010 alone, but not all of these businesses worked under the same legal structure.

If the size of a business doesn't determine their legal structure, then what is an LLC? An LLC, or limited liability company, is one type of business entity that allows the business owner to have fewer tax difficulties with the same legal protections a corporation would have.

So how do you determine whether or not you should be forming an LLC or starting a corporation? It all comes down to what you would like covered and protected by the law.

LLC vs Corporation and the small-business owner

There's a reason why LLCs are often presumed to be small businesses. This is because it's typically easier for a small business that has a limited number of owners for an unlimited amount of time. For instance, family businesses where the business is intended to pass down from the parent to the child over a period of time may find running an LLC to be an easier legal choice.

However, an LLC may not be the best choice for every small business either. It may be a better idea to start your business as a corporation if you have multiple people buying stock from your company or if you have outside investment offers.

Benefits of an LCC

There are many benefits of being a member of an LLC. Benefits include protection of the business owner's assets should a fault result in a lawsuit, a more relaxed requirement for tax filing, and the ability to file for business taxes on one's own personal income tax return.

It may be a challenge to convert your business to an LLC if your business isn't being built from scratch. However, this is also determined by the state in which you are converting your business to an LLC. Fortunately, the challenge of converting to an LLC is predominantly found in the transferring of assets from one type of legal entity to another.

Many businesses in their beginning stages tend to use the benefits of an LLC because of the legal precautions that exist. LLC advantages also allow for the running of your business without the hassle of tax and financial burdens.

Exploring the benefits of forming your LLC In delaware

If you're forming an LLC or corporation, you may know that one of the biggest decisions you need to make involves where it will be based. Each state has different laws and regulations regarding the operation of LLCs and corporations, but many people choose Delaware when they're setting up LLCs for a number of different reasons. Here are just a few benefits of an LLC in Delaware.

Series LLC states

There are eight different states that offer the status of series LLC, and one of them is Delaware. A series LLC works well for businesses that work with rental properties; it essentially allows an LLC's assets to be divided into different sectors to eliminate the risk of one particular asset from taking on damages or liabilities if a different asset is lacking in performance. Delaware was actually the first state to allow series LLCs, and they're a safer and more protective classification in many situations.

Freedom of contract

Delaware is also one of the states that allows the members of the company to dictate the overall structure of the company and tailor it to their specific needs and goals. The contract is called the LLC Operating Agreement, and all members should give their input when drafting it. Experts say this is easily the biggest benefit of starting an LLC over any other business type.

Lower annual fees

Unlike other states, Delaware has an annual Franchise Tax Fee of just $300 for LLCs. A form must also be filed once a year with the Delaware Secretary of State to update any changes or essential information. Finally, the registered agent must pay a small Registered Agent Fee, since all Delaware LLCs are legally required to designate a Registered Agent to accept legal documents and services.

Ultimately, these are just a few of the many Delaware LLC benefits. When considering starting your LLC in Delaware, it's important to understand that there are three rules an LLC name needs to follow,

including: being different from an existing LLC in the same state, must indicate that it is an LLC, must not include words restricted by the state. Keep an eye out for the next post, where we'll discuss even more advantages of setting up LLCs in Delaware.

In the last post, we discussed some of the essential advantages to forming an LLC in Delaware over other states. According to the National Association of Small Business's 2015 Economic Report, the majority of small businesses surveyed are S-corporations (42%), followed by LLCs (23%), and many big-name LLCs choose Delaware as their designated state of operation. Here are some more Delaware LLC benefits.

More confidentiality

One of the benefits of LLCs in Delaware is that it offers a higher level of confidentiality. It can be a real advantage for business owners who prioritize privacy. When the LLC owners are creating the rules for their specific business, a document must be filed, called the articles of organization, or sometimes referred to as the certificate of formation. And while all states make this document available for the public to view, Delaware has one advantage in that the document does not have to reveal the names and addresses of managers and members.

Enhanced court system

Many business owners choose to start an LLC in Delaware because its court system is well known for being favorable to business owners. the Delaware court system has a specialized type of court that is designated to solving business conflicts, called the Court of Chancery. Legalzoom.com says, "under Delaware's LLC law, the Court of Chancery's jurisdiction includes LLC disputes. In fact, members of a Delaware LLC have the same right as shareholders of a corporation to file a derivative action in the Court of Chancery; that is, a lawsuit to enforce an LLC's claim against another individual or company that is not being adequately pursued by the LLC's managing members."

More favorable taxes

When you start your LLC, one major decision you'll have to make is whether you want it to be taxed as an S corporation, a C corporation, a sole proprietorship, or a partnership. In Delaware, LLCs with one member are not legally recognized by the IRS, so they don't have to pay any taxes at all — it's all passed through to the owner.

Ultimately, understanding how the advantages of forming an LLC vary from state to state is integral to having a successful business structure.

About MyUSACorporation

Since 2010, MyUSACorporation.com has been paving the way for clients around the globe to incorporate, providing the keystone upon which numerous brands have built and prospered.

"We've built our success by giving others the tools and foundations they need to be successful," says owner and CEO Julia Greenberg-Aguilar, "The incorporation process can be confusing and intimidating, especially for foreigners, so we make the process easy."

Upon her arrival in the USA in 1995, the Ukrainian-born immigrant immediately embraced the American Dream and set about learning all she could. She "had all kinds of jobs," she said, "from bartender to working as a buyer for the biggest vending company in the region." Her diverse experience gave her a unique perspective on the challenges faced by entrepreneurs of all types.

In 2010, Greenberg-Aguilar joined MyUSACorporation.com as a manager, and quickly moved up to partner in 2011. Her unique insight and passion for helping her clients earned her a peerless reputation and, by 2017, she had taken full ownership of the company.

As many entrepreneurs find, the process of structuring and incorporating a business is fraught with pitfalls that range from a bureaucratic, hard-to-understand administrative process to outright scams designed to prey on those charting unfamiliar business territory.

"There are so many contradictions, the process is not straightforward at all," she said, "registering your business with the state is not the same as getting a business license, and getting a license doesn't include a tax ID." She continued, "And that's just the start. Business structure, tax structure, all of it can be catastrophic for a startup if you don't set it up correctly."

Navigating that intimidating landscape is where MyUSACorporation.com really excels. Greenberg- Aquilar and her company have helped tens of thousands of entrepreneurs with setting up and dissolving their businesses, obtaining proper licenses and tax IDs, certifying business documents for domestic and foreign use, and much, much more.

While online incorporation services aren't scarce, MyUSACorporation.com distinguishes itself through a commitment to quality and service, with a-la-carte pricing friendly to startups who are often on a budget.

But that's far from the only way MyUSACorporation.com stands out.

Herself an immigrant, Greenberg-Aguilar provides special attention to her international customers. Many incorporation services hesitantly provide minimal services to foreign clients, but MyUSACorporation.com embraces them, taking special efforts to fill the unique needs of non-US entrepreneurs. Virtual US mailing addresses and embassy certifications are just a few of the tailored services available to clients, and services are available in numerous languages such as Spanish, Ukrainian, Mandarin, Cantonese, and Russian.

This attention to the international market has paid off, too. After serving more than 10,000 clients in the first four years, MyUSACorporation.com plateaued before seeing skyrocketing growth under Greenberg-Aguilar's leadership.

This growth opened opportunities for the company to expand, onboarding Julia's daughter, Katerina Zuniga, in 2017 into the role of general manager. Katerina, who was born in Ukraine and moved to the US at age six, holds a bachelor's degree in Business Administration from Fordham University.

Her minors in Finance and Marketing and specialization in International Business made her a perfect fit for continuing the MyUSACorporation.com journey to becoming a premier business services powerhouse.

"Having the right team, the right knowledge and the greatest respect for your clients is the recipe for success," Greenberg-Aguilar said.

Today, MyUSACorporation.com has enjoyed explosive growth, and the needle is still going up. The company is in the final stage of unveiling an all-new website with automations and services specifically designed to enhance the customer experience. "You have to aim for the best customer experience in the industry," Greenberg-Aguilar reiterated, "that's how you keep growing."

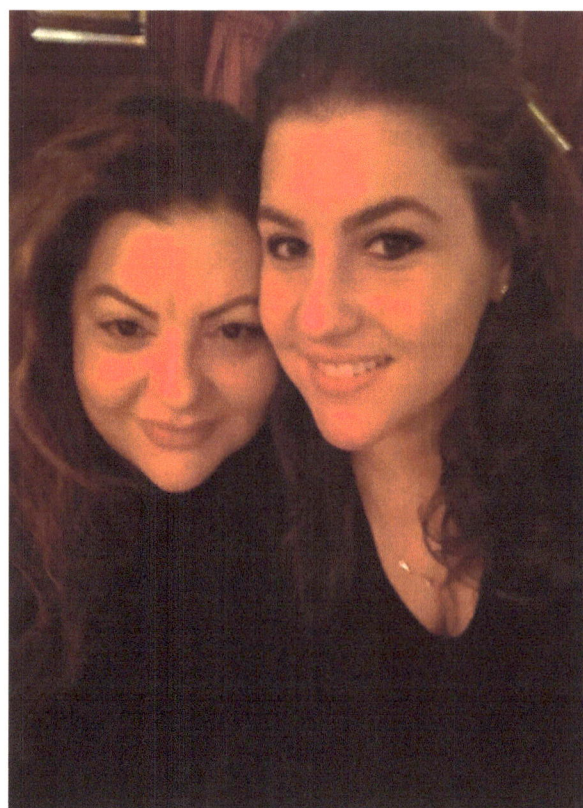

Reach New Customers with Automated Retailing

> **The challenge for companies and brands is to find cost-effective ways to expand distribution, reach and inform new customers, and build awareness in a scalable, affordable manner.**
> – Bob Bienias, Vice President, The Venders

There are numerous challenges facing companies and brand managers these days. There is a proliferation of competitors in most categories, leading to decreased brand loyalty. The amount of choice people enjoy today allows customers to switch brands as well as retailers or online stores from purchase to purchase, depending on which best serves their needs at the time.

Additionally, old-school retailing is simply not what it used to be. Retail has one of the highest employee turnover rates, and since the pandemic, many people simply don't want to work at low-paying jobs. There has been an entire cultural shift in attitudes toward employment.

The fact is, finding and retaining staff is one of the toughest challenges, and replacing employees requires a lot of time, energy, and cost.

The good news is that the pandemic pushed customers out of their comfort zones and in many cases, forced them to shift their buying patterns. This made them more open to discovering new channels and brands.

An insightful report from McKinsey shows that since the onset of the pandemic. a whopping 75% of consumers have tried new brands, places to shop, and shopping methods.

This presents a unique opportunity for companies looking to expand reach using new, cost-effective solutions.

Automated retailing provides new and established businesses the ability to reach new customers virtually anywhere— without employees. Moreover, these systems can attract customers with sight, sound, motion, and emotion through interactive graphics and videos; educate and inform curious customers; and sell 24/7 without you every having to lift a finger.

The system does all the work and allows you to track sales through an online portal.

Additionally, with automated retailing, start-up time is measured in days, not weeks or months. You will start generating cash faster than with virtually any other business.

You can be an absentee owner or a hands-on operator. Because you can monitor the business from any computer (or even your phone), you can engage fully in the business or manage it from a distance.

By now, you're probably wondering if we are simply selling a vending machine. The answer is no. There are plenty of companies that will sell you a big vending machine that is equipped to dispense snacks and sodas.

Our automated retailing systems are completely different. They don't even look like vending machines.

These technologically advanced systems are designed to fit almost anywhere and take up just two square feet, so they can adapt to virtually any environment.

What can you sell out of these automated systems?

Our clients have had great success selling items ranging from CBD products and vapes, to cosmetics and personal electronics, and thousands of other types of merchandise. Best of all, in certain categories, we can supply the inventory as well as the automated retailing machine, making this a true turn-key value.

With our relationships with brands across the world, we not only can supply the automated retailing system, but also, in many cases, with the inventory. The eliminates the need to find and manage a supply chain, which is especially critical in these days.

Our recommendation for businesses and entrepreneurs to start close to home, assuming that home is a midsize to large city, and go slow. Start with just five machines to get the feel for the business. After a couple of months, add another five, and then scale up as you wish. You can literally make as much or as little money as you want. If you desire a bigger paycheck, put out a few more machines.

Now, of course nothing is quite so easy. There is some work that needs to be done, including finding the best locations for your machines (which we can also help with). But within a short time, you'll be an expert at noticing the purchasing patterns in your area (you get daily reports on what's selling), and you will know just how to maximize sales and expand your business.

And believe it or not, many people don't want to become millionaires. They just want a nice steady income they can depend on, and they don't want to focus on continuing to grow a business. And that's fine, too.

Bob Bienias brings a wealth of senior management experience through his prior association with White Consolidated Industries and Electrolux manufacturers and distributors of major appliances throughout the US.

Before being one of the driving forces behind the development of The Venders, Bob acted in a consulting capacity to several entrepreneurial and industrial firms, either launching new products or maximizing the sales of existing product lines.

Content is Queen

Kelli Maxwell

Content marketing. Content is king. We hear those phrases often, but what is content marketing truly? Simply put, content is the creation of photos, videos, memes, blogs, or captions that people put into the online world. Marketing is the act of making others aware of it. Content is the information we all consume online, in our news feeds, and in the ads that stalk us incessantly.

Gone are the days of old-school ad agencies facilitating big spends on television, radio, and newspaper. Just a few decades ago, only the titans with a hefty budget could afford to advertise and get their message into the world. Social media completely leveled the playing field for everyone. Anyone can have a voice, anyone can build a brand, and anyone can attract their audience with the content they put out; without even spending a dime.

When was the last time you listened to the radio and endured hours of ads? Most of us would rather pay the fee on a streaming service, never listen to a paid ad again, and not even notice that we are inundated on social media with messaging. This is because it comes across as authentic content that entertains us, engages us, or educates us. It resonates with us or elicits an emotional response, and we appreciate the time that company took to speak directly to us.

Our world was recently rocked by a pandemic, an election, and several changes to the way we are able to advertise digitally and who we can target. Yet one digital marketing principle remains true- content is still queen.

It's human nature to look for the easy way out. To find automation and processes that replace human interactions and the time spent facilitating them; to work smarter, not harder. But we seem to be forgetting one thing. The most important thing: Humans do business with HUMANS. Not bots, not funnels, not automation, and definitely not spam messages, emails, and ads.

Especially now, when consumer privacy is paramount, the way you attract people online to your brand is of the utmost importance. It's found in the content brands are putting out on social media platforms. Is your content generic, boring, and irrelevant? Or is it authentic, bold, pushing the boundaries between following advertising guidelines while still being hilarious or profound?

The ad agencies of old did one thing exceptionally well. They cared about PEOPLE. They wined and dined their clients. They spent time with them outside the agency. They got to know who they truly were as people and why they cared so much about their brands. They invested thousands into learning which ads would speak to their audience while also honoring their client's personal beliefs and philosophies. It was an art that has not been lost on the content creators of today.

Social media took that away from us for a time. We became impersonal, used filters to hide our true selves, and only posted the highlight reels of our lives to elicit envy and jealousy from others. But now, especially now that we've survived the last few years of lockdowns, restrictions, and division amongst ourselves, we crave connection more than ever. This is why authentic content marketing will always emerge victorious.

No matter what we go through, humans are wired for connection to other humans. No matter how many dollars we make through bots and automation, if all of that were stripped away, I'd hope we'd still have relationships and people to see us through the hardest of times.

How are you connecting with your people? As the landscape of marketing changes yet again, I urge you to utilize your voice online, through social media platforms, to spread your message in an authentic and unapologetic way that attracts your audience, keeps them engaged with your brand, and connects with them in a way that no other form of marketing can do.

Kelli Maxwell is the CEO and Founder of Ember Marketing Group based in Billings, Montana. Kelli is nationally known as the "Content Queen" and has an innate ability to authentically amplify her client's brand and voice through the content she and her agency create for them. Learn more at embermg.com

KWE
PUBLISHING, LLC

How Being a Veteran-Owned Business Can Help You Grow Faster

It is estimated that there are more than three million veterans in the United States. Many of these men and women have sacrificed much for their country. They have served in the military and put their lives on the line to protect us and ensure that we have the freedoms we enjoy today.

Veterans have earned a reputation for being hardworking, honest, trustworthy, and reliable. That's why it makes sense that they would want to start their own business and build a successful business for themselves.

What is a veteran-owned business (VOB)?

A veteran-owned business is a business established by a person who has served in the United States armed forces. These businesses are recognized as eligible for certain tax breaks and are given special treatment when seeking financing.

There are four types of VOB companies:

1. Small business
2. Women-owned business
3. Service-disabled veteran-owned business
4. Disabled veteran-owned business

Six reasons why VOBs are successful

These companies have a higher success rate compared to other companies.

These companies also have several advantages. They are better at handling unexpected changes and disruptions in the market. They also have better cash flow, and they usually have lower operating costs.

1. Flexible hours

When you work for a large corporation, you usually work 9 to 5. For VOBs, this is flexible, and employees can work whenever they need to. It is helpful because it allows them to work during off-hours and also makes it easier for them to meet deadlines.

2. Low fixed costs

A large corporation has high fixed costs. These include rent, insurance, taxes, utilities, salaries, etc. Because of this, they

have to raise their prices to cover these costs.

On the other hand, VOBs do not have fixed costs. It means they can offer lower prices because they are not paying for rent, insurance, and taxes.

3. Access to capital

Because of the low fixed costs, VOBs often receive better terms when it comes to financing. They usually have better access to capital.

4. Better management

VOBs are typically run by veteran entrepreneurs who know how to manage a business. When you run your own business, you are responsible for everything that happens. It means that you can make mistakes and learn from them.

5. Strong customer service

VOBs have a history of providing excellent customer service. They know how important it is to provide quality products and services. In addition, they also understand what customers want.

6. Increased employee loyalty

When you work for a large corporation, your employer often pays more than what your job is worth. On the other hand, VOBs pay a lot more than average salaries. It means that employees are more likely to stick around.

Why you should be a veteran-owned business

Here are some of the reasons why you should be a veteran-owned business:

Better Quality. Veterans tend to know what they're doing because they have spent time serving the country. They are also often more honest and hardworking than non-veterans.

Loyalty. Veterans understand what it means to serve their country and will likely stick with their businesses.

Efficiency. Veterans tend to keep their businesses running smoothly and efficiently. Non-veteran business owners often have difficulty learning how to run a business, and they may not be able to keep their business running properly for as long.

Savings. Veteran-owned businesses tend to be more profitable than other businesses. They also tend to offer discounts to military personnel, which helps their bottom line.

Reliability. Veteran-owned businesses are usually more reliable than other businesses. They often have more experience in working with government agencies and contractors. They also tend to be better at delivering products or services on time.

Reputation. Veteran-owned businesses are usually well respected by the public. They tend to work closely with the government to know what it takes to get things done.

Support. Veteran-owned businesses often receive exceptional support and assistance from the government. They are also more likely to have robust support systems in place.

Access. Veterans-owned businesses have access to specific government programs that other companies do not have. They also get access to preferential pricing on particular products and services.

Stability. Veteran-owned businesses have more stability than other businesses. They are less likely to go out of business. They also tend to stay in business for a long time.

Trust. The public and government agencies trust veteran-owned businesses. They have earned this reputation through their quality work and loyalty to the country.

How to start a veteran-owned business?

Step 1: Determine if you have what it takes

Are you the type of person who can run a business? Do you have what it takes to start a business? Do you have what it takes to be successful? What do you need to become successful?

Step 2: Develop a business plan

Create a detailed business plan. It can be a simple list of steps to follow or a more complex project. If you're having trouble coming up with ideas, think about your goals. What are your goals? What's your best business approach?

Step 3: Find a mentor

Find someone who is already running a successful business and ask them for advice. It will help you learn from their mistakes and successes.

Step 4: Get financing

Do you have enough money to start a business? Do you have what it takes to get financing? What are your options? What are the risks?

Step 5: Determine your location

Determine where you want to start your business. Do you want to start your business in an urban area? Do you want to start your business in a rural area? Do you want to start your business in the suburbs? Do you want to start your business in a particular state? Do you want to start your business in a specific country?

Step 6: Determine your product or service

Determine what type of product or service you want to offer. Do you want to sell products or services? Do you want to sell a product or service you already made or created? Do you want to sell a product or service that you don't currently make or create?

Step 7: Determine your marketing strategy

Determine how you're going to market your business. How are you going to get your customers to know about your business? Do you have a website? Do you have social media accounts? Do you have a Facebook page?

Step 8: Get your business license

Do you have what it takes to get a business license? Do you have what it takes to start a business? Do you have what it takes to get financing? Do you have what it takes to find a location? Do you have what it takes to determine your product or service?

Step 9: Determine your startup costs

What are the equipment and supplies you need? Do you have what it takes to buy these items? What are your startup costs?

Step 10: Determine your startup time

Determine how long it will take to start your business. How much time will you need?

How to create an effective marketing plan for your veteran-owned business

Marketing is vital to growing a successful business. Creating a marketing plan that attracts potential customers takes time, money, and effort. In today's economy, where small businesses compete with giant corporations, knowing how to market your business effectively is essential to standing out among the competition.

Creating a marketing plan

The first step in creating a marketing plan is deciding what you want to accomplish with your marketing efforts. It is a crucial step because it helps you determine if you should create a formal marketing plan. A good marketing plan will include details about what you want to accomplish, such as increasing revenue or making new contacts.

Next, you must decide how much of your marketing budget you are willing to allocate to each of your goals. Spending at least 10% of your marketing budget is essential to reach your long-term goals. When creating a marketing plan, writing your expectations for each campaign is also helpful.

A final step in developing a marketing plan is determining whether to hire a consultant or work with a company that specializes in marketing.

Marketing plan components

Once you have created a marketing plan, it is time to determine what components will make up the plan. You should divide the program into three sections:

Target audience

It is a list of people you hope to reach through your marketing efforts. You should include the demographics of your target audience, such as gender, age, income, and geographic location.

Campaign ideas

It would help if you brainstormed ideas for each campaign. Think about how you can get the word out about your product or service. Some movements are simple and require little effort. Others will require more research and planning.

Campaign strategies

You should also determine the methods you will use to promote your product or service. It includes where you will advertise, what you say in your ads, and how often you will run your ads.

How to avoid pitfalls in starting a veteran-owned business

A recent survey revealed that almost half of the VOB owners reported encountering at least one major problem during their first few years of operation. One-third said that they had to close their business. These problems include:

1. Inadequate financing. The most common financing challenge was insufficient capital. Almost half of the VOB owners had difficulty finding financial support for their business. And only 28 percent found a lender willing to help them get started.
2. Poor business plan. More than half of the VOB owners unable to secure adequate financing had trouble developing a viable business plan.
3. Too many regulations. Although VOBs are exempt from federal regulations like the Small Business Administration, they must comply with state and local laws.
4. Lack of awareness. Many VOB owners didn't know about the Servicemembers Civil Relief Act. The act provides several tax breaks and other benefits to qualifying veterans starting new businesses.
5. Excessive red tape. VOB owners face red tape and a long government approval process when starting a new business.
6. Too many rules. Many VOB owners have had to hire a lawyer because of the complexity of federal and state regulations.
7. A lack of support. As a result of the high costs of starting a veteran-owned business, most VOB owners are not supported by the VA.
8. Poor management. Many VOB owners have been frustrated with poor management at the VA. They are often left to operate a business while the VA pays their employees.
9. Loss of investment. Because the VA does not guarantee VOBs, they do not qualify for the VA guarantee. As a result, the VA does not reimburse the owners for their losses.
10. Long waiting times. Most VOBs take a year or more to begin providing goods and services. The lengthy approval process means that VOB owners may be forced to close their business before they start getting any revenue.

Benefits for veteran-owned businesses

The SBA has several programs specifically aimed at benefiting veterans and their businesses.

- VetBiz Loans. The SBA offers loans and grants to small businesses owned by veterans and service members and to small businesses in targeted distressed communities.
- Section 8(a) Program. The Section 8(a) program helps veterans obtain financing for their businesses. The program offers incentives to

banks and lenders to lend money to qualified small businesses.

- Veteran-Owned Small Business Administration Certified Service Contract program. This program provides guaranteed contracts for certain types of small businesses.
- Women Veteran Owned Business. This program assists women-owned small businesses in obtaining contracts.
- Section H11 Small Business Innovation Research Grants. Grants are available to assist small businesses that develop products, services, or processes that benefit the warfighter.
- Small Business Innovation Research program. Grants are available for research and development projects that benefit small businesses.
- Section 8(a) Loan Guarantee program. Grants are offered to financial institutions that make loans and loan guarantees to small businesses.
- Microloan Program. The SBA provides microloans to small businesses to help them start and grow.
- Veteran-Owned Small Business Development Center program. Grants are provided for training and educational programs to assist small businesses owned by veterans and service members.
- Veteran-Owned Business Development Center Program. Grants are provided to eligible small businesses for programs that enhance their ability to expand, diversify, and create jobs.

5 Questions Every Founder Must Ask

If you're a founder or CEO of a startup, you've probably heard the term "founder's dilemma" used a lot. It's a term that refers to the fact that you have to choose between the interests of your investors, employees, customers, and yourself. But it's not just a dilemma for founders—it's a dilemma for anyone who owns a company.

The last few years have been a whirlwind for entrepreneurs. It's become easier to start a business, but the challenges that arise along the way are just as difficult to overcome. As a founder, you'll find yourself trying to juggle the many responsibilities of running your business. In addition to that, you'll also be responsible for your company's success. So, you must make sure you're asking the right questions and getting the answers that will help you make intelligent decisions.

What are five questions every founder must ask?

There are so many things founders need to consider before they start building a business. Before they begin developing a product, they should ask themselves the questions. It is what I am talking about today.

Here is the list of 5 questions every founder should ask themself.

1. **What is my idea worth?**

In case your idea is not something valuable, it means that you won't be able to raise money, and you won't be able to do a business out of it. If your idea is not valuable, then you should not start working on it.

If you think your idea is valuable, you should talk to your investors and start pitching them. They may fund your idea or not. But you won't know the answer if you don't ask them.

2. **Who will be the customer of my product?**

As a founder, you should find out who will be your customers and how you will sell your products to them.

Let's say you are building a social network for bloggers. You should know that bloggers are going to be your customers. Also, you should figure out how you will get paid for your product.

3. Will I be able to get people to use my product?

Another important thing you need to consider is whether or not you will get your potential customers to use your product.

If you are selling a new product and no one is using it, then you won't be able to get anyone to use it. If your potential customers don't use your product, you need to work on it and find a solution.

4. Do I have an MVP ready?

If you don't have an MVP ready, you should start working on it. You should focus on your product's core features and functionality.

If you don't have an MVP, you should start working on it immediately. Otherwise, you won't know if your idea is going to work.

5. Is my idea good enough to get funding?

Now, it's time to get funded. There are many ways to get funded. You can get funding from investors, angels, friends, family, and others. If you have a product ready to launch, you should get it funded as soon as possible. Otherwise, you will have to wait for a long time.

Here, you should ask yourself if you have an MVP. If yes, you should find out whether you have a product that will be funded.

What risks and sacrifices does such an enterprise demand?

As far as the risks are concerned, they could potentially be huge. There is no way to be sure that everything will go according to plan and that nothing will go wrong. As you know, there are risks associated with every decision that is made. However, there is a lot more risk involved in this purchase than you might think.

A big issue is that the vendor has been purchased, and they are now the ones making all the decisions. It is not necessarily bad, but it can make it hard for you to get things done if you're not paying attention. They might decide without thinking of the consequences that could occur. For example, maybe they choose to move forward with a new feature that they really want to implement, and they don't think about the fact that the site would become unstable for the customer.

The most significant risk is not being able to get any support. It would be impossible to get help from the vendor because they are the ones who designed the product. It would be nice to have some free support or pay per incident, but it isn't possible.

There is a risk that they may change the pricing structure. There are lots of good products out there for free, which could impact your company's purchasing decision. It wouldn't be fair if the vendor suddenly changed the price, so they are no longer the cheapest option.

Setting strategy: How will I get there?

As we begin our journey together, you have a lot to look forward to. First of all, you'll have a solid foundation to build on. Then, you'll be able to learn all you need to know about yourself, including your strengths, weaknesses, and personal preferences. You'll be able to develop your career path and build skills that will help you move ahead in your career. You'll be able to improve your life, your health, and your relationships. You'll be able to gain the confidence you need to live out your dreams.

You're so close to starting your new life. But first, I want to share my top three strategies to help you get there. These strategies are meant to be used alongside each other. They're not separate from each other. They work hand in hand, so make sure you use them all.

1. Be clear on what you're aiming for

Be clear on your vision for yourself. What do you want your life to be like? What do you want your career to be like? What are you going to accomplish? What are you going to do?

Please write it down. Write out your goals, your desires, and your aspirations. Make sure they're specific, measurable, and realistic. You can use the SMART goals checklist to help you. If unsure, you can ask a trusted friend or family member.

Next, identify the steps you'll need to take to achieve those goals. For example, if you want to start your own business, write out your plan for what you need to do to get there.

2. Know your strengths and weaknesses

The next step is to identify your strengths and weaknesses. These are your core areas of strength. They're the areas where you're most likely to succeed. They're the areas where you're most likely to grow.

If you don't know your strengths and weaknesses, you won't be able to identify your career path. You'll have no idea where to go, how to get there, or what you need to do. So, take some time to identify your strengths and weaknesses. You can use this self-assessment tool to help you.

3. Identify your personal preferences

Finally, you'll need to identify your personal preferences. It is the area where you can shine. You'll be able to work with your strengths and weaknesses.

In addition, you'll be able to choose the right job. You'll be able to work in the field that you love. You'll be able to work for a company that aligns with your values. You'll be able to work in a role that makes a difference.

Your personal preferences include your personality type, preferred work environment, desired lifestyle, and ideal job. You may also want to consider your interests, hobbies, skills, talents, and passions.

Can the strategy generate sufficient profits and growth?

Business strategy is the process of making a plan that involves the vision, mission, objectives, goals, and strategies. It is tough to develop a business strategy because it requires a lot of planning and time. The business strategy plays a significant role in every stage of the organization. Business strategy is an essential part of the business plan. Without having a business strategy, it is impossible to manage the business.

Hence, the company needs to have a business strategy.

Strategies are divided into two types: long-term and short-term. The short-term strategy is based on current events and is related to the immediate future. Long-term plans are based on the past. These strategies are developed after analyzing the market trends and identifying the competition. Hence, a good business strategy is necessary for the company to survive the tough competition. A good business strategy increases productivity and reduces the risk of failure.

To know whether a company has a strong business strategy, it should be analyzed on the following points:

1. The vision should be clear and provide a future direction
2. The mission should focus on the purpose of the company
3. The goals should be clear and measurable
4. The objectives should be realistic and should be achievable
5. The strategy should include a plan of action for success

12 Creative ways to fund your startup

In today's competitive world, one has to do everything to get an edge over their competitors. You must be thinking about what to do to fund your startup.

Startup funding can be done in many ways, and here are 12 such creative ways to fund your startup:

1. Crowdfunding

The primary source of funding for most startups is crowdfunding. It is a popular fundraising method in which many individuals contribute small amounts of money to the project.

2. Angel investors

Angel investors are people who invest in startups for their own financial gain. They are usually venture capitalists, private equity firms, and angel investors.

3. Venture capital

Venture capital is a pool of investment capital that is invested in startups to finance growth and expansion.

4. Personal loans

Personal loans are also a good option for funding your business.

5. Bank loans

Bank loans are a great way to fund your startup. It's a loan with a fixed interest rate and repayment schedule.

6. Credit card

A credit card can be an excellent way to fund your startup. The card companies usually charge a low monthly fee or give you a sign-up bonus for using their card.

7. Investment

Many investors would like to invest in your startup. These people would like to make a profit, but they also have an interest in the company's future.

8. Sell stuff

Selling Stuff online is a perfect way to make money. Whether you sell Stuff like digital cameras, watches, accessories, gadgets, etc., you can quickly get paid by buyers. You can start selling things on eBay, Craigslist, Amazon, Etsy, etc. Here is a good article on how to make money on eBay.

9. Debt

Debt can be a good option for funding your startup. But it would help if you considered getting into debt with a high interest rate.

10. Freelance for others

Are you an expert in something? Maybe you are a graphic designer, a copywriter, a programmer, etc. Freelancing allows you to offer your services to others who need them. You can work for clients or work for yourself.

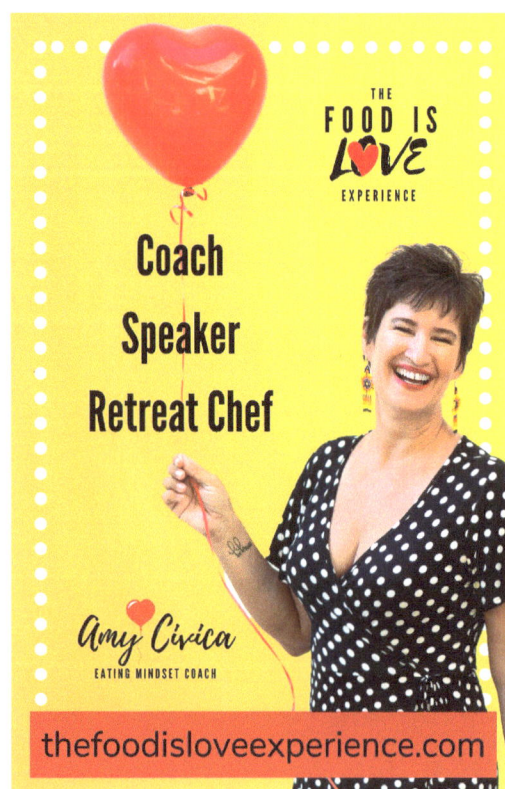

11. Sell products on Amazon

Selling products on Amazon is another excellent way to make money. You can market your products on Amazon if you have any particular expertise.

Many people are making a full-time income by selling their products on Amazon.

12. Crowd-sourced capital

It is a variation on crowdfunding. Instead of asking people for money directly, people are asked to invest in your company. Crowd-sourced capital is a great way to get funding for a startup that has already developed a prototype. The company will give a share of ownership to investors, and the investors can either sell these shares for a profit or hold on to them for the future.

You need to ask yourself a series of questions before you start your business. The answers to these five questions will help you create a great business plan. The best way to get to know your customers is to talk to them. The more you understand your customers and their problems, the easier it will be to create a product or service they will love.

Successful Leadership in a Remote Workforce

Successful Leadership in a Remote Workforce matters most! Time and budget permitting, remote workforces are all the rage. They eliminate the need for expensive office space, fuel costs, time-consuming commutes, and wasted hours waiting for coworkers to show up. It's also easier to find talented remote workers than ever.

Here are tips on managing a remote workforce:

A remote workforce is not a "regular" workforce

It's tempting to apply existing management techniques to remote teams. Resist that temptation. While there are similarities, managing a remote workforce is different – so different that any advice you hear about managing a regular in-office workforce might be useless or even detrimental if applied to your remote workers.

Be an alumni mentor and coach

It's easy for a manager to feel disconnected from his employees if they work remotely. Having a single manager, who also happens to occupy the same physical space as his workers, can help mitigate such feelings of disconnect. It's best if that manager is someone the team members were previously in regular touch with and can act as an alumni mentor and coach.

Be the manager you want in ten years

Once you've been down this road—which you will be—you'll know what to do. You'll see that you should have been doing things differently from the get-go to be successful. So take that knowledge, apply

it to the next step —hiring and recruiting remote workers, and become a leader.

Have a stand-up meeting if you must

Any meeting is better than none, but some stand-up meetings can be stimulating for a team if done properly. They are like game shows where everyone is playing for prizes.

Take holidays

Remote workers may be very different from in-office workers in some respects, but they are just as human. They need breaks too, so let them have them.

Listen to what people want

Your workers might love remote work because they want to spend more time with their partners, kids, and other family members, travel the world or be a practical way to earn money while having fun and pursuing their passions.

Cultivate remote-friendly policies

Companies will find it easier to hire remote workers if they have a culture of openness and acceptance. Allow people to work when convenient for them, not just when their employer is paying for the time.

Automate your job

Don't let the notion of remote work overwhelm you. Every company needs someone to manage their technologies and systems, so if you can manage most aspects of your workflow digitally, do so. Not all tasks still require human interaction, so take advantage of those.

Prove others you can do remote work

If you've been in remote work for a while, there's no way people will believe you can still be productive. Keeping up with a workday demands different time management skills than when you were concentrating on an in-office workforce. So the first step is to prove that your remote workers can keep up with everyone else at the office.

Be flexible

If you can't trust your remote workers to be available, don't hire them. And if you need to have someone at the office for certain functions, such as weekly meetings, video conference in with them via video chat or a phone call rather than employing them. If it's impossible to do that, then don't get rid of the satellite office. It might save you money in the long run since your employees will be productive and happy working remotely.

Know your company's culture and expectations

Company culture will influence how a remote workforce is managed. Some companies are very open and flexible, and others are less so. For example, many startups have a culture where remote work is not encouraged since it can be disruptive to employees' work-life balance. How a company handles remote work will also depend on managing the in-office workforce.

Take things online

Please don't ask your remote workforce to go into the office for meetings simply because you want to see them. Use technology to bridge any communication gaps. Treat virtual meetings as in-person meetings to get the same results.

Understand time zones

Time zone differences are not trivial, and both managers and employees will benefit from learning about them. Make sure your remote workers know the time zone differences between their office and their place of work. It's best to meet in the middle so that you can communicate with them while they're working, and they will be available to you at a moment's notice.

Be available to your remote workers

Just because you're not there doesn't mean they don't exist or aren't important. Make sure your employees are connected to a live person on-call 24×7. Be available to them, and don't let your remote workforce feel alienated.

Keep an in-office manager

If you're going to have remote workers, you need someone in the office who understands them. Some people baulk at this idea, but it's not that difficult to make a manager who oversees the remote workforce feel at ease with the arrangement, and it will help your managers to learn how to be more flexible.

Stay on top of task and project management

If you haven't used a project management system before, now is the time. Ensure everyone on staff knows what they're working on and what they should be doing. Use your task and project management software to assign tasks, deadlines, and due dates. You can also add discussion threads for issues that need to be discussed and suggestions for new initiatives.

Know when to make changes

Some remote workers will be very independent and capable, while others will need more support. Use your resources wisely. If you determine that a remote worker is not up to the task, you must let them go. The same goes for any in-office workers who are not meeting expectations.

Force virtual meetings

No matter how great video conferencing technology is, it will only work if your team uses it. Invest in a virtual meeting room and let your remote workforce know that meetings will be held there. That way, you can take advantage of the technology and maintain a connection with everyone in your team.

Improve your communication skills

Since you won't be in the same room as your teammates, communication will be more challenging for you than if you were at the office together. Don't try to force it, but be sure you have clear, honest, and constant communication with your remote workers. Communicate as much as you can in writing or by phone. Schedule a meeting rather than show up on their doorstep if you need to meet face-to-face.

Provide communication tools

Even if you have a great relationship with your remote workforce and are in constant communication with them, there will be times when they will have to contact you. Your best option is to provide Skype, Google Voice, and other VoIP options so they can contact you when they need to. If they're not comfortable with that option, consider giving them opportunities for leaving messages or call-back procedures.

Share expectations

Saying that you're going to do something doesn't mean you should do it. Make sure everyone understands what is expected of them and what isn't. If they don't understand, then explain it to them. Then check with them again to make sure they know and know the consequences of not fulfilling their responsibilities.

Do what you say

You're setting an example for your remote workers. Make sure you live up to your communication standards and keep the lines open with them. Don't say one thing and do another. Show that you'll be honest with them, and they'll be honest with you.

Be open to honest feedback

Sometimes a little push is all it takes to get remote workers rolling in the right direction. If they have a problem, talk about it and see what can be done differently to improve the situation in the future.

Benefits of remote workforces

In an increasingly competitive and global economy, leaders in any industry are looking for ways to maximize their employees' strengths. One of the most effective methods for doing so is through remote workforces.

1. Remote workforces are growing globally

"It's no secret that remote workforces have been more prevalent for a few years now, but it's only recently that this trend has picked up the pace and become a recognized practice. With social media reaching all corners of the globe, even geographically isolated individuals communicate with one another in ways that would've been impossible even a decade ago," according to Business News Daily. In fact, according to a 2015 Gallup poll, 47% of American workers said they regularly worked from home.

2. Remote workforces produce stronger results

In addition to being more prevalent, working from a remote environment can yield stronger results than traditional office environments. In fact, according to a study published in the Harvard Business Review, employees that work from home are more productive than employees that work in office environments. Employees reported working 8.5 hours per day when working from home and 7.6 hours per day when working from the office. The study found that employees in a remote workforce are more productive because working from home encourages employees to be more "self-directed and less distracted by coworkers."

3. Remote workforces encourage constant communication

Because remote workforces are not limited to a specific geographic location, they allow employees to communicate at any time, encouraging constant involvement in the workplace and among teammates.

According to the Gallup poll, "79% of those who work remotely say they at least occasionally connect with team members outside of their usual work hours, compared with just 29% of those who do not work remotely." It is a beneficial aspect of remote workforces because it encourages constant communication and involvement.

4. Remote workforces encourage diversity

Since most remote workers are Millennials, they have a unique perspective on how business is conducted. According to the American Psychological Association, Millennials are described as being more: open, global, and self-expressive, and they have grown up using technology that expands their sense of what is possible. Since they have little experience with 9-to-5 work environments, their time is fragmented, their loyalty is less likely to be tied to an organization or group, and they are less committed to long-term goals.

5. Remote workforces promote availability

Because they are not limited by traditional office hours, remote workforces encourage employees to set their hours and make their schedules. "Because remote workers are not tethered to the office, they can be more flexible with when and how long they work," said Adam Tickell of FlexJobs. "This allows employees more freedom in how and where they work, making them more available."

6. Remote workforces encourage flexibility

Since remote workforces are not restricted by office hours, employees who work from home can manage their time to work best for them. "For some of us, working from home means we can take advantage of the flexibility to start earlier or finish later if our tasks allow it," said Pam Woods of LearnVest. "It also allows us to be more productive during the daylight hours when we have more energy and feel most effective."

7. Remote workforces help employees develop skills and strengths

Working from a remote environment can allow employees to explore their strengths and develop new ones. According to the Harvard Business Review, "The capacity to work remotely is an asset that companies can use to help employees work through the risk of failure and the discomfort of self-doubt."

8. Remote workforces can lead to a better work-life balance

Working from home allows employees to balance their work and personal lives by working when convenient. "It means you have the flexibility to create your schedule, whether that means waking up early to take your kids to school, taking an evening class, or working a more traditional nine-to-five schedule."

What it takes to be successful

If you're thinking about establishing a remote workforce and you've been considering the challenges, here's what it takes to be successful:

- Clear expectations and boundaries with your team, which are communicated at the outset of working remotely
- A culture of openness and mutual trust that fosters effective collaboration between team members in different locations, on different schedules
- Fostering trust over time by understanding what motivates individuals to be successful: individual recognition for achievements, opportunities for personal growth and development
- Building an organizational culture that. fosters a culture of performance, an environment in which people, who embrace the values of the organization and have demonstrated their ability to contribute, are being promoted

- Being able to find uplifting human connections among team members who originate from different cities (or locations)
- The ability to rise above the challenge of distance and work long-distance by staying connected as much as possible, seeing teammates as often as possible, and using technology where possible
- Establishing effective communication with team members located geographically or in time zones that are far apart
- Establishing the principle of self-discipline for the team by making sure team members are aware of the goals and encouraging them to monitor their progress toward meeting those goals, keeping tabs on projects that take too long or have not been completed working with them towards achieving results
- The ability to take on a team role to support team members who are located geographically or in time zones that are far apart
- Knowing when it's necessary to ask for assistance when something can't be done and how to be proactive in seeking assistance from colleagues

Servant Leadership Principles

Michael Sipe

What is Servant Leadership?

Purpose: Serving The Majority. The "maintenance and care" of the people, the culture, the business, and that method is the Servant Leadership principle that provides the foundation for all of its principles.

The Servant Leadership principle focuses on the principles and practices that sustain a successful group. The team leader must be a servant, a Servant Leader, and a servant-leader.

When we talk about professional development, leadership skills are a core component. Quite often, the leadership training focuses on the external outcomes of what is labeled as "good" or "poor" leadership. However, when leaders focus solely on the collective growth and performance of the team, they often miss opportunities to be self-aware of how and why they acted or led the way they did as a manager.

Servant Leadership Principle 1: Listening

To be a fantastic pioneer, you must first be an excellent audience. The ability to listen is a center correspondence ability. It is critical to the success of any initiative.

Servant Leadership Principle 2: Empathy

Empathy is the second principle in the SERVANT-LeadershipTM acronym. To lead others, you must understand what it's like to walk for miles in their shoes.

Since you've never been in their shoes, you should have the empathy to see their situation through their eyes.

Servant Leadership Principle 3: Healing

A working group should be "entirety" on an individual and aggregate level, as indicated by Greenleaf, in case they will perform successfully. Worker pioneers encourage conditions that help the

physical, mental, and passionate prosperity of every individual they lead. Take a blow at underlining growth and completeness in your group building works out, for instance, and in your discussions with people.

Servant Leadership Principle 4: Self-Awareness

In discussing the principles of servant leadership, the one principle that gets overlooked the most is the area of self-awareness. A leader naturally needs to be aware of their team, their performance and who they are serving at-large. Yet from an individual level, in order to truly no our

capabilities as a leader, we not only need to look at the outward sense of things. We need to look at inside ourselves.

One's ability to connect with one's inner self can bring clarity to problems and can encourage reflecting on the past choices and their respective outcomes to find future resolution. When we know our habits, our repeated patterns of behavior, our reactions to specific events, we serve ourselves best by reflecting on why we chose what we did.

Self-awareness means looking at the thoughts and emotions that led to those actions and seeing them for what they are. Fear can be a paralyzing and restrictive force. If we don't see that a form of fear was there in our thinking when we made certain decisions, then we are bound to repeat the same response in the future. There are often latent fears or subconscious thought processes that will tie us up and keep us from making better decisions as a leader.

A leader who is not only thoughtful about their employees, should also be thoughtful about their own thoughts and behaviors. A leader grows in ability when they see the impact of their choices from the prevalent thought process they had at the time. They become aware of how and why they make the choices they do.

Here's the wonderful thing. When they ask "why," nine times out of ten they will say, "How can I do that better?" or "How could I have handled that differently?" When they do this, they accelerate into growth mode as a person and especially as a leader. Each time they are more aware, they create a higher consciousness and bring a better version of themselves.

They learn that their poor choices may have adversely affected their team and they can stand strong in voicing their shortcomings with the team. Then move to make a better choice in the future. This gains greater trust from subordinates because they see not only that they are expected to improve but their leader is also making valiant strides in improving their personal and professional self in the form of leadership.

Becoming self-aware creates the window of opportunity for growth. All leaders must continue to grow and including an active practice of being self-aware is an essential component to being a great servant leader.

Servant Leadership Principle 5: Persuasion

It is called servant leadership because the leader is more compassionate and modest in his or her dealings with their subordinates. The conventional connection between management and workers is being challenged by servant leadership.

Servant Leadership Principle 6: Conceptualization

It is a management style that emphasizes what the leader can offer their company or organization and Community. Focuses primarily on the wellbeing and growth of people/communities they belong. The leader shares the power helps develop the people first, put the needs of others and perform as highly as possible.

Servant Leadership Principle 7: Foresight

Leaders with foresight are able to learn from both the past and the present. Their understanding of the ramifications of their actions will improve as a result of these teachings.

Servant Leadership Principle 8: Stewardship

Servant management is or have to be the bedrock of all corporations. It's some distance based on the principle of increase through individual recognition and fulfillment. The idea is that through a selected set of practices leaders can pinpoint the strengths and weaknesses of the corporation and the personnel to better balance overall performance.

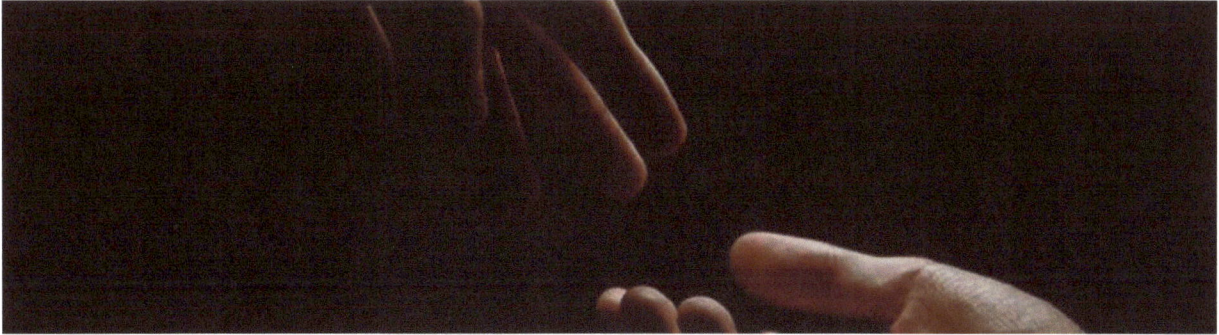

Servant Leadership Principle 9: Commitment to the Growth of People

Servant leadership is a leadership style specifically designed to empower employees. Unlike traditional leaders, servant leaders focus on the development and growth of their employees, not just reaching the organization's goal.

Companies generally promote productive and helpful employees, not those who exist to advance the organization's goals. Leaders are in charge but care about how work gets done and are more concerned about the people they're leading.

Servant Leadership Principle 10: Building Community

You know the whole concept of servant leadership is a paradox. It's an idea that the leader will serve other people, but at the same time, the leader is going to influence other people. To sum up, it is a style of management that puts the team's development and well-being ahead of the organization's or leader's objectives. So, servant leadership starts with the idea that you want to serve and do good to others.

Advertisers

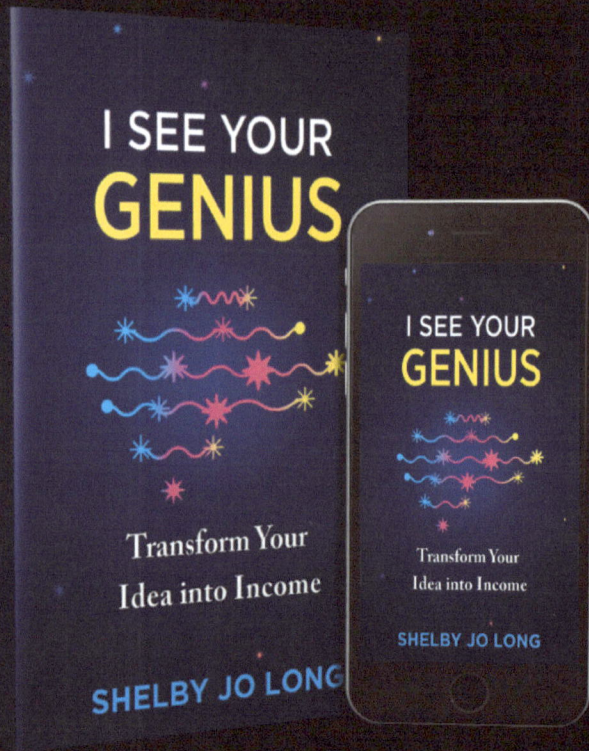